USA TODAY BESTSELLING AUTHOR

K WEBSTER

Paused to Prolific

Cover Design: All by Design
Photo: Adobe Stock
Editor: Kim BookJunkie
Formatting: Champagne Book Design

From *USA Today Bestselling Author* K Webster comes a quick guide to help you **write faster**, **stay focused**, and **avoid burnout**!

With over eighty published titles (and counting), K Webster is often asked how she remains prolific and successful. She'll reveal in a humorous, yet effective, manner how she keeps her focus and has managed to publish one or two stories each month consistently for over five years.

In this easy-to-read book, you'll learn to retrain how you think and new habits to help you become productive in a few simple ways by:

Identifying Your Problem
Making a Plan
Being Accountable
Staying Focused
Sticking to a Schedule
Staying Productive

Using short exercises in each section, you will begin to understand how to put into practice what you'll learn in this book.

This is a quick and effective 12,000-word guide meant to cut through the fat and get straight to the meat so you can get back to writing!

For Mr. Webster—

You married the madness and live to tell the tale.

CONTENTS

NOTE TO THE READER

I hope you enjoy my fun and helpful take on how to stay focused and get words under your belt. Everyone is different, but I'm hoping you'll find some of the practices I use helpful in your own quest for success. If you're reading this book, then you're looking to improve the way you do things. I'm confident that if you read this book with an open mind and test out some of these methods, you too can begin to increase your writing productivity. Give me an hour of your time, and I'll give you the tools you need to write all the words!

Good luck!

K Webster

INTRO

Writer's block. It's the excuse for the slowing, the pausing, and the ultimate stopping of the words that are locked in our brains. A crutch. Two dirty words. Something foul and hated by every person who's put pen to paper to try and exorcise the demons in our heads.

But blocks are just that.

An impenetrable force standing in our way that keeps us from our ultimate goal: our story.

Blocks can be destroyed. They can be climbed. And they can be stepped around. Thinking of your writer's block tangibly, you can break down the dynamics of your own block so that you can make a plan to figuratively get around it.

If you take anything away from this book, I hope that you'll learn more about yourself, exercise some tactics to create better habits, and get back to writing. We'll take "coffee breaks" along the way, so you can pause to consider your own process and personality to help understand what hinders and motivates you.

Before you embark on this introspective journey, sit back and relax. Unplug and reflect. Think back to the beginning when the characters were clawing to get out and you had an equal amount of eagerness to obey them and the bravery to do them justice. That first book—*maybe it's still inside that colorful brain of yours, but you're working to get it out*—is a reminder of your *purpose*. I'm willing to bet, back then, you weren't motivated by money or popularity or acceptance from your peers. Back then, it was all about the story.

So, let's do what we do best.

Tell that story.

Since I can't hear about your first, I'll tell you mine. Later, you can tell the tale of your first story to someone else. It's good to be reminded of your starting point—when you first hit the ground running—since that's going to be the fire you'll tap in to when you're sputtering on fumes.

For me, I was inspired after a book signing I attended as an eager reader. During the entire two-hour drive home, I thought about characters and a story that spoke to me. Since the drive was boring, I daydreamed about what my hero looked like, what my heroine smelled like, what their conversations sounded like, and so on. By the time I made it home,

I was burning with the desire to write the story that had unfolded like a movie in my head. I sat down, opened Word, and typed out my first book in ten days. The book was just over 50k words, not long to some writers, but significant to me back then. Those were 50k words I didn't have the week before. A story was born. My little book baby came kicking and screaming into the world, and I couldn't have been prouder. I won't go into my publishing journey because that's not what this book is about, but I will tell you what I did right after I typed those glorious words "The End."

I started again.

And again.

And again.

For five years straight, I've written and published over eighty books. I've learned strategies that work and waded through some horrible advice that didn't. Eventually, I found what works for me. When you finish this book, I think you'll find what works for you too.

Enough reflection, let's find out what's blocking you and smash it!

Identifying Your Problem

IDENTIFY WHY YOU'RE STUCK

"*I'm a terrible writer.*"

"*I suck.*"

"*My words are crap.*"

"*Why do I even try?*"

First of all, let's get one thing straight. There are good voices in your head—ones who give birth to characters and stories—and there are the bad voices who kill your vibe, flatten your characters, and murder your hope. It's time to analyze which voices are speaking loudest then put them in their appropriate corners. You're going to home in on those good ones, the ones that create, and we're going to let those "squirrels" run wild.

"But I'm a planner, K. I work in an orderly environment. Everything has a place and a plan."

If that's true, great, you have it all figured out. Keep trucking along. However, I don't think you'd be reading this book if what you've been doing is working for you. Face it, ***Squirrel Herder***, you're here because you need to move blocks, so you can go on to moving mountains.

Right now, you're probably stuck on the fact that I've called you Squirrel Herder. Good. There was a point to that. Think of all those voices bouncing around, tugging you this way and that way, as squirrels. Name them. Discipline them. Reward them. Once you become familiar with them, you can begin to sort through them, and uncover what's truly blocking you on your quest to finish your book.

"No voices in my head, K. I'm just stuck."

Stuck on a feeling.

Tired. Hungry. Sad. Angry. Hurting. Anxious. Depressed. Overwhelmed.

I get it. Truly, I do. I wake up tired. I go to bed amped up. I'm a whirlwind of twenty-seven different feelings sucking my energy all at once. It's exhausting.

You may be blocked because you can't get in the mood to write. You're going to learn to manipulate your mood.

Coffee Break*—Write down the top three moods or feelings that prevent you from writing. For me, it's fatigue, stress, and distractibility. Feel free to write more than three. For now, we're simply analyzing what's stopping us and putting it on paper.*

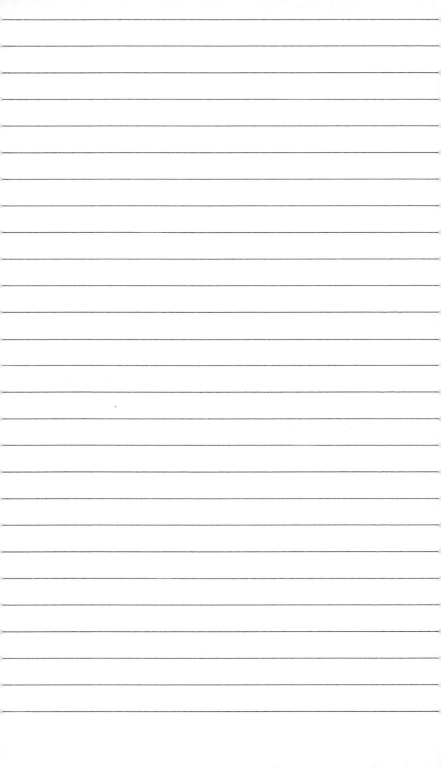

Distract

Squirrel Herder, *—that's you in case you forgot*—I'd like to introduce you to ***Ooh, That's Pretty! Squirrel***. This one's a wild one. A sassy little beast. This bouncy little squirrel will sift through your moods and direct you when you're lost. She'll pull you from your most difficult mood and drag you to your happy place. She'll hunt out every shiny nut for you to marvel and drool over—anything to cheer you up and make you forget your current state of blah.

Instead of squirrelling out over any ol' thing, you need to fine tune these moments into periods of planned distraction. Let every trip away from your manuscript be a mission to refuel, to circle back around and come back to it soon.

Ooh, That's Pretty!

So, you're mad, you're sad, or you're about to fall asleep on the toilet because life is catching up to you. But your book demands your attention. You need to get words down. With every step you take away from your computer, the guilt threatens to suck you under. So, stop swimming against the current, and go with the flow.

You need a vacation.

Where are your characters? Are they at home? A beautiful location? Big city or a small farm? Wherever they are, you're going there too. I find the best visual samples come from Pinterest, but you can use Google if you're feeling frisky. One quick search and you're inundated with pictures of exactly where your characters are at. Start an inspiration board, and save these pictures because when you're feeling uninspired, they'll be a quick pick me up.

You need to laugh.

Memes. Jokes. Quotes. Whatever reminds you of your characters and story, you should be saving those too.

You need to see your characters.

Who are they? What or who do they look like? Who do they sound like? Hunting down pictures helps keep the characters alive in your head.

"But, K, this is silly. I'm supposed to be writing…not whatever this *is."*

You're missing the point, Squirrel Herder.

The point is, in order to find your writing mojo,

you need to learn how to reprogram your mind. This entails finding inspiration and motivation when you're not busy tapping away on the computer. When you're not writing and you want to be, you should be using that time to mentally inspire yourself to write.

Coffee Break—*Start an inspiration board for the story you're working on now. If you don't have a story you're writing yet, start one for the story you want to write. Pin pictures of locations, vehicles they drive, character inspiration (pictures you find that remind you of your characters), foods your characters eat in the book, clothes they wear, jewelry, etc. Once you have them pinned, scroll through them all, and you'll start to feel the vibe of the story as it comes to life before you.*

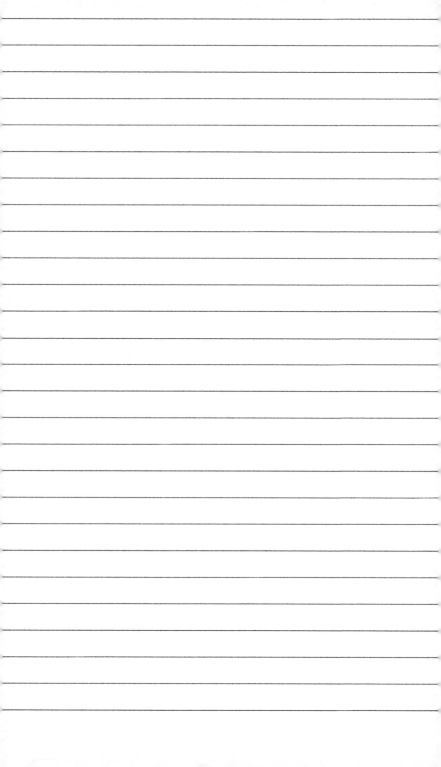

Decompress

Sometimes, no matter how much you distract your mind with pretty things, it doesn't matter. When this happens, you'll need to step away from everything. I do this often, but usually after a hard day's worth of writing.

I read.

I watch television.

I sit quietly and think.

I look out the window.

I draw.

I walk. Just kidding. I really don't walk, but if walking is your thing, do it.

The point is, your squirrels are stressed out. They need to rest or play or daydream. You, Squirrel Herder, are in charge of taking care of these sweet inner beings. Don't starve them of the things they need in order to thrive. We all need a moment to walk away, decompress, and hopefully come back stronger.

"But, K, whenever I sit down to read a book, it makes me want to write."

"K, when I see that hunk on television, I think about Hero Harry from my story."

Ahhh, now you get it. That's it! Deprive your characters and your story a little bit longer while you give your attention to someone else's book or someone else's characters on television. Feel that burning? That intense need to get back to YOUR book?

Good.

Harness how that feels, and learn to watch for it. Learn to poke at it and taunt it. Remember, you're retraining your thought process here. I, personally, play psychological mind games with myself all the time in all aspects of my life. I'd rather not question the reasoning behind this, I'm just glad it gets me the results I want.

By allowing your brain to decompress, you allow those lines of creativity to open up once more. People often gasp when they find out I read a book every day or two in addition to writing as much as I do. Reading helps me decompress, and it fuels me on. A bonus to decompressing is when I read other people's books, it encourages me to become a better writer. This isn't a time to compare how much better they are than me, but a time to appreciate that I can aspire to be more.

"But K, I can't write while I'm reading someone else's book. It's too confusing."

Great, Squirrel Herder, but you aren't writing all the time. And a chapter here and there isn't going to do damage, trust me. It'll do more good than harm. This is about you trying new things…so try them.

However you choose to decompress, do it with purpose. Give your brain a break by tricking it into wanting to work. When you find things that particularly motivate you, put extra focus there.

Coffee Break—*Snag a cup of joe or your favorite tasty beverage then jot down five things that have nothing to do with writing that makes you decompress. Don't have five yet? Include things you're willing to try that might relax you. Here's my five: listen to music, scroll on Pinterest, watch horror movies, read alien romances, daydream quietly. Save your list as a reminder, and keep it handy, so you can pull it out when you're staring at a blank screen and need to step away to reset the mind.*

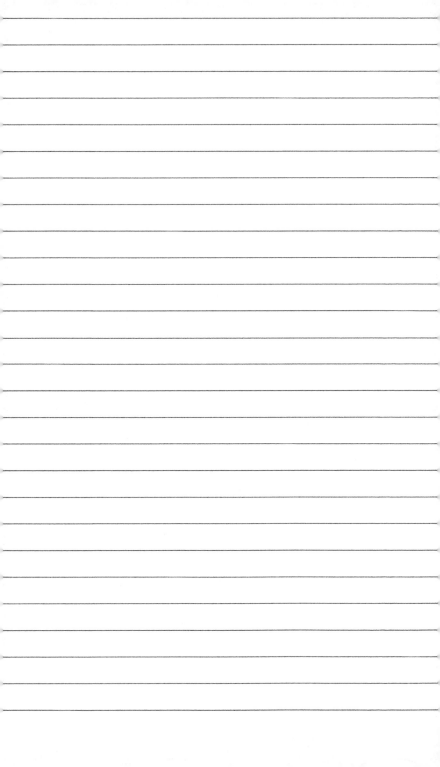

Making a Plan

BRAINSTORM

Writer's block is sometimes as simple as getting stuck on a scene, a character's motivations, a plot hole, etc. You may have spent hours or even days stewing over this, but that's all in the past now. There's an easy way around writer's block.

First of all, there's the literal way around it: You can step around the block and skip the scene until it comes to you. Some people have no qualms about writing out of order. For the other half of us, this is terrifying.

"But, K, what are the ripple effects?"

"What if skipping the hard scene now means I paint myself into more of a corner later?"

"This book is in pieces now, and it'll never come together."

Squirrel Herder, get ahold of yourself! No one said write the entire book, just start writing past what's blocking you. We'll get into more of that soon, but first, let's address those concerns.

You can't move on?

Then let's dig a trench and fight against this block.

"K…"

Hold on to your britches, soldier. We're not going to war. What we're going to do is put our thinking caps on. Brainstorming is critical in moving past writer's block. Critical. So critical that we're going to have to pull in our most creative squirrel.

Meet ***Brainstorming Betsy Squirrel***.

She's loud. She says everything on her mind. Words fly from her lips. Nonsense. Utter nonsense. Whines. Complains. Ponders. Exclaims. Brainstorming Betsy Squirrel plucks out every thought pertaining to your story and tosses them in a pile. The heroine could die. The hero could take up knitting. Aliens could invade. Here's where you start throwing out silly, outlandish ideas then start weeding through them to find the clever, brave ideas that are hidden amongst the pile. Your story isn't supposed to be boring and predictable, but it feels that way to you making you not wanting to inch forward, not even a little, for fear of writing too far into something that you'll want to scrap later. That's why you're stuck. You know what you *should* do, but it's not what you *want* to do. Brainstorming Betsy Squirrel agrees that you need to get it all out on the table before trying to make sense of the madness.

"I can't walk around talking to myself, K."

Ehhhh. You can't? Well, if you're not comfortable with that, call your cat into the room. Visit Grandma. Look in the mirror. Facetime your bestie. I brainstorm most successfully when I'm on the phone. All it takes is a good, trustworthy listener on the other line, and I let all the thoughts fall out, so I can then sort through them. Sometimes, my husband gets this job. While he's not the greatest listener—*often giving me plot twist ideas where everyone dies in the end*—he's excellent at being a sounding board while I rant. It's as if the moment I start speaking about my characters, the storyline, or my struggles, that my excitement begins to outshine my fear or frustrations. And though he usually offers unique ideas that I'd never personally write, it kick-starts my own mind to rearrange things into a path that finally makes sense.

This works.

I've been stumped countless times, and a quick brainstorming session has pulled me right out of the funk. I not only manage to get past the difficult chapter or scene, but I then have the drive to finish the rest too.

Sometimes, it takes several brainstorming sessions in a row to really get the story back on track. I tend to take less notes during these times, spending more of my energy playing this new movie (the things I've brainstormed about or the new book I'll write) in my head, so that I can see it clear as day.

If you're not brainstorming during your times of struggle, you most definitely need to be. The cat may not be ideal because he doesn't talk back, but you don't technically need someone to respond for this exercise to work. You just need someone to listen, even if that someone is your face in the mirror.

If you have a person who is a great listener and offers feedback, you've won the writer's lottery. My brainstorming session friend will sometimes say one line that unlocks the entire mystery in my head. When I'm obsessing over a key element and can't move past it, an outsider's eyes can see the obvious fix to my problem. Then, I'm able to hit the ground running again.

This is my favorite tool against writer's block, and once you learn to utilize it for yourself in a way that helps you, it'll be your favorite too.

I mean, who doesn't want to ramble for an hour about their book and force their victim to listen to their disconnected madness right as it pours from the source? Some people play Candy Crush for fun, others babble incoherent thoughts to their friends, hoping it results in a book in the end. Everyone has their thing...

Coffee Break—*Brainstorm a story idea for practice. It doesn't have to be one you ever plan on writing, this is just to get you used to talking things out. Talk to the cat, a spouse, your sister, a friend, the neighbor, the wall. I do this often. I call it exorcising my demons. Not only will this help you later, when you're brainstorming to get over your writer's block, but you may find a new story hidden inside of you. By talking out some stories I wish I could write but will never have the time for, I get them out of my head and into a quick outline…just in case. After your brainstorming session, jot down some notes and save them in your bank of "book maybes" for a later date!*

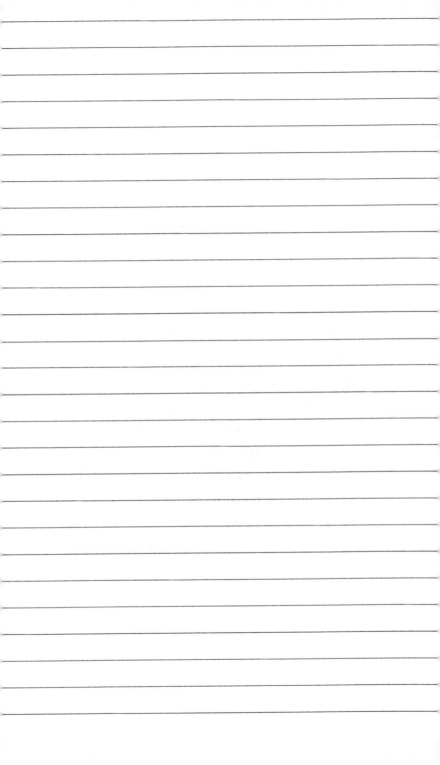

BREAK IT DOWN

Sometimes, writer's block occurs because you're obsessed with a certain part of your story that you want to write but just aren't there yet. I tend to write chronologically because I'm a little bit obsessive about order. So, when my brain becomes fixated on that first intimate scene, when the villain dies, when the big twist is revealed, or the sweet epilogue, I tend to slow, sputter, and stop during less exciting chapters or scenes. For me, the 30k mark is where I begin to question everything.

Is this book boring?

That's the one that screams at me every time. I'm nodding off, thinking about lunch, or wishing I could curl up in bed to read instead. When this happens, I worry that if my story is so boring even I want to run away from it, imagine how it'll be for the readers.

Listen really well…

Your book is probably ***not*** boring.

Lunch sounds good and you're probably hungry, but that doesn't mean your book isn't at exactly the right spot and where it needs to be. I've questioned myself at this point so many times, and sadly enough, I've dropped projects at this mark.

Now, you can stop and go shopping, nap, or do whatever calls to you, or you can wrangle your squirrel to get him to work for you, Squirrel Herder. Work smarter, not harder.

Meet ***Bang-Bang Squirrel***.

Bang-Bang Squirrel is out of control. He's a fire starter. A feisty one. The furry little beast loves sex, drugs, and rock and roll. He's here for the highs of the book. Climaxes, explosions, drama. He wants to be right in the middle of all of it. This particular squirrel gets restless during the emotional scenes or the necessary but quiet ones.

Rather than ignoring this energetic furball, give him what he wants. Give him a cup of coffee and a handful of firecrackers. Let him blow stuff up and create excitement.

"K, you're telling me to skip the pivotal scene where Hero Harry watches Heroine Holly write in her journal from afar, wondering if she's scrawling out her undying love for him?"

Sorry, what's that? I fell asleep three times reading your question.

Yes.

That scene is important, but you're bored and not writing it anyway. What I'm telling you is to skip to the part where Hero Harry finds the journal, takes it to his room, and reads all the sordid details, his door open and Heroine Holly in the other room where she can catch him in the act at any moment. It's okay to fast forward to the part where she discovers he's spying on her and she throws a vase at him if that's the part you're itching to write.

Skip to the juicy bits.

It'll get you writing, and that's the goal of this entire book. Once you're fired up from writing that scene, you can circle back and really give the "pivotal scene" the meat and purpose it needs to get you to the exciting one you just finished.

Recently, I needed to get a story written in a 3-week period of time. The pressure was killing my mojo. Rather than throwing in the towel and pushing back my release date or forcing myself to stumble through what I saw as the boring (but extremely necessary beginning), I skipped to the middle.

The middle was the love story and that was the part I was feeling.

Humans are fickle, emotional creatures. Often, we do best when we don't fight our instincts, but go with them. In this case, I dove into the love story and wrote something epic and powerful. When I finished, it was easier to go back in and fill in the necessary beginning to lead to that magical romance. Then, I rolled right through the end without issue. While I don't normally like to write out of order, I'm learning that desperate times call for desperate measures. We can change our patterns of thinking and processes with practice and trial and error. You never know until you try.

Coffee Break—*Write a one page scene about something dramatic and wild. Perhaps it's a scene you wish you could have included in a previous book or something you'd never normally write. Let Bang-Bang Squirrel light the scene on fire with something fresh and exciting. Get to know how this feels and how it feels to give in to it. The purpose is to get those juices flowing, and the added benefit is you can use what you come up with as a bonus excerpt in your newsletter or the start of a new book!*

ORGANIZE

Whether you're a pantser or a planner, you'll want to pay close attention to this section. Organizing your thoughts isn't the same as outlining your novel, it's much simpler than that. So that you can focus on your writing, you need to condense your ideas into a quick, easy to follow, short list. I tend to organize my thoughts in my iPhone's notes app, limiting them to a few paragraphs, summarizing the key points.

Rather than getting lost in a giant book of notes when I'm trying to write, I keep my notes app handy and type a couple of comments on the document to keep my train of thought focused on the general gist of my novel.

Once the notes are in place, I like to go ahead and fill in the chapters. Then, I add comments to each of those chapters—just a sentence or two taken straight from my notes to keep me on track in each individual chapter. I have an idea of where to go, but also plenty of wiggle room to chase story squirrels if need be.

"But K, I'm an extensive note taker."

Okay, Squirrel Herder, that's wonderful. I think there's a cookie with your name on it somewhere. But for the purpose of this book, I want you to try something new. Take the time to read through your notes or outline extensively when it doesn't interfere with 'writing time.' But then, I'd also like to see you condense those notes into a more succinct format that you can move quickly from. Think of it as an outline for your notes, brief and just something simple to jog your memory.

"How do I condense twelve pages of notes into four paragraphs?"

Magic. Or.... practice. Just keep playing with it until you get it in a way that clicks in your mind.

These organized notes will also help you when you're working on multiple projects at once. They're a quick breadcrumb trail you've left for yourself so that when you're writing is interrupted, it's not so difficult to come back to it.

Coffee Break—*Outline one of your current WIPs in just a few quick paragraphs. Or, you can choose a new story to do this with. Then, open your Word document and break those notes down into chapters with comments flagging each chapter. This is so you can get a feel for how it should look.*

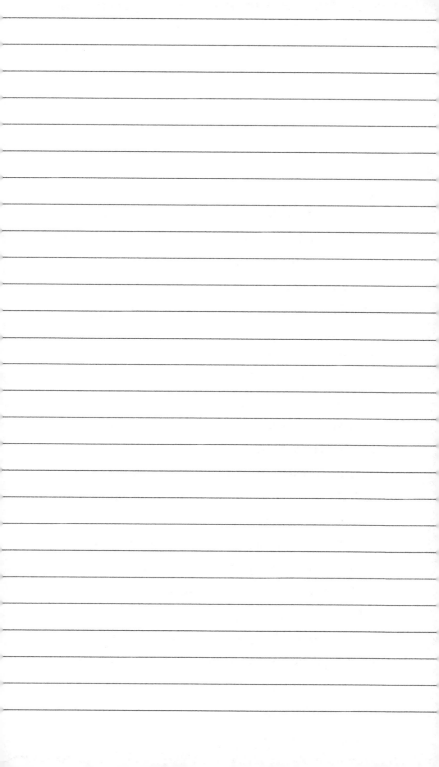

SET THE SCENE

I like to be romanced…into writing that is. Just like every oddball writer out there, I have particular foods, sounds, seats, etc. that set the perfect mood for an ideal writing environment. Before I learned to set my scene, I'd sit in my chair, edgy and twitchy, making excuses just like you probably do.

"I can't write today because I just don't feel right. Something's off, K."

Of course it is. This isn't a fairytale with talking squirrels who save the day…okay, so maybe it sort of is. You just need to to identify what's off and learn how to get it back on track. That "off" feeling is anxiety or fear of starting. If you succumb to these feelings, you're setting yourself up for failure before you've even started.

This is not the time for checking to see how many likes the picture of your dog wearing sunglasses got on Instagram. This isn't time to sort out why your cable bill seems higher than last month. This isn't the time to text back and forth with your sister over what happened on the latest episode of Outlander.

No, this time is for you to set your scene with a little help from a friend, Squirrel Herder.

Meet ***Grammy Loves You Squirrel***.

This squirrel is like your grandma. She's accommodating and wants you to be happy. Her entire goal in life is to make sure you're fed, cozy, and doing what makes you smile. Let her make you your favorite drink, let her tell you how cute you are despite not having showered for two days, and let her tuck you in with the softest blanket in the house. Whatever your "scene" is, let Grammy Loves You Squirrel help you find your writing zen. Once you do that, like the sweet furball she is, she'll leave you alone, only coming back to refill your coffee and remind you to take bathroom breaks.

Identifying your scene is the first step in recreating it over and over again.

Find your favorite blanket, your lucky writing socks, and fill up your cup of go-go juice. Turn on your tunes and settle down at the computer. Whatever it is that gets your creative juices flowing, makes you physically comfortable, and puts you in your happy writing place, get it. Then, don't look at email or Facebook or Photoshop. Don't do anything but look at that open manuscript staring you in the face.

Now type.

Your scene is set and you need to type.

All the icky feelings of the real world—I know, I cringed too—will start to melt away as you immerse yourself in the world of make believe. Everything around you in your perfect scene will fade into the background as you become one with the keyboard.

So, stop sitting there squirming and frustrated. Set your scene, get that computer open and ready, then dive in. It's really that simple. The hardest part is the first jump, but you'll be swimming in no time.

Coffee Break—*Jot down your ideally perfect writing scene. Location. The song that's playing in the background. What you're wearing. The drink you're sipping or the food you have ready to snack on. How comfy is the chair? Now, learn to set your scene before you sit down to write. Only have two hours before you need to go to bed? Get your scene ready then dive in. Waiting for the perfect conditions to come about will only put off your writing. Instead, create the perfect conditions without hesitation. Make it routine. For me, I prefer to be dressed for the day and sitting in my recliner under a blanket. I want a fresh cup of coffee. I need to have just eaten because I don't like to snack while I write. The house needs to be completely silent. Such a simple scene to set. Work on yours!*

Be Accountable

ACCOUNTABILITY

It's time for you to be accountable for your actions, or in this case, your inactions. These methods are easy and effective. All it takes are some caring friends and a little due diligence on your part.

"I sprint, K."

That's lovely, Squirrel Herder. Fantastic. Keep sprinting if that helps you get down those words. I want you to write them down.

"My sprinting group has a document where we all add our word count."

That's great too. But you also need your own document. One that stays on your own computer that you visit daily.

There was a time when I'd track my word count for the day, but never recorded it anywhere. My small (or large if I was killing it that day) victory was short lived, though, because after a few days, I'd forget how well I'd done that day. Then, when the end of the year rolled around, I had this desire to know how many words I'd written in the past twelve months. I'd spend hours hunting down each manuscript, adding together the word counts.

That was messy and time-consuming.

Make yourself a spreadsheet. A word count tracker. Or, download K Webster's Paused to Prolific Word Count Tracker for free. I want you to keep up with this daily, so keep this document open at all times. Daily accountability is crucial in your success. It gives you a big picture look at your writing rather than only a daily snapshot. When you're feeling low because it's been ten days since you've written anything, you can look at your spreadsheet and see that overall, you have written words, and today or tomorrow might be the day you start recording more. Don't be afraid of the zeroes. Let them motivate you. You shouldn't care what all the authors around you are doing because you're only competing with yourself. You're outdoing what you did yesterday or last month. Only you have this data to use to your advantage. No more sitting on the sidelines, upset that you have nothing, because that's not true.

At the end of the year, you will have an entire spreadsheet filled with 365 days of numbers, even if some of those numbers are zeroes. If you can fill each day with something as small as 200 words a day (you're talking two paragraphs or so), that adds up to 73k words in a year. Begin with 200 words a day baby steps and you'll soon have yourself an entire book.

Coffee Break—*Jot down how many words you think you write in an hour. Then, keep a tally of what you actually write in that hour (keep going if you're on fire, but also keep in mind what stops or slows you down). Eventually, you'll need to upgrade to a daily spreadsheet, but the purpose of this exercise is to get you used to tracking your writing speed. If you notice anything slowing you down or stopping your writing process, make note of it. You might recognize patterns/behaviors/issues you can change or identify things that need to be removed from your scene.*

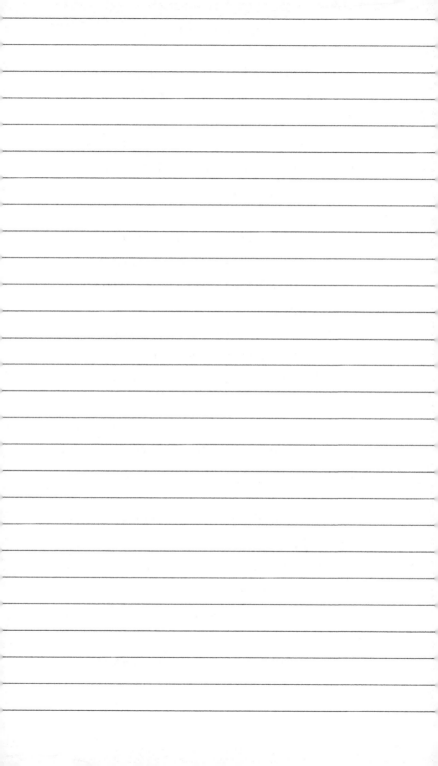

Writing 200 words a day is awesome, but I want to help transform those 200 words a day into 2k. With my methods, this can easily be done. I know, because I've done it year after year. There's no magic. No ghostwriters. No gimmicks. Just focus and rewiring your stubborn brain.

Meet ***All-Star Squirrel***.

This fella is fast. Dedicated. Motivated. But most importantly, he thrives on showing his team what he can do, that they can depend on him to complete his tasks. All-Star Squirrel is badass, but he can't win the game on his own. He needs help from his cheerleaders, coaches, the other players, and his fans. We all have the All-Star Squirrel inside of us waiting to come forth and perform, but like any great athlete, he needs a team to help him realize his full potential so that one day he can be dedicated, quick, and focused.

All-Star Squirrel's cheerleaders are insanely supportive and positive. There are people in your life who fit this bill. Utilize their pep and turn them into proverbial pom-poms. Share your daily successes with them. Let their praise motivate you to write more.

"But, K, I don't have any cheerleaders in my life."

You have someone. Whether it be an online peer, a spouse, child, your neighbor, or your granny. I always tell my husband about my daily word count (even when it's zero), and he tells me, "That's good. Now write more."

Which brings me to All-Star Squirrel's coaches. They're the gruff ones, the whip crackers. The realists who remind you that you're not going to make it to the finish line by pushing out daily zeroes. They push you when you don't want to be pushed, and they remind you of your goals. These people are every bit as important as the cheerleaders.

Now, this brings me to other teammates. These are your peers. The busy little writer bees who are also doing what you're doing day in and day out. They're on your team because they play the same game, and you support one another. The other players are the ones you get on the field with and put your heads together to talk out the plays. Discuss the nitty gritty. The stuff that's never meant for the fans to see. Don't compare yourself to the other players. They have different roles, level of experience, or areas of expertise.

Finally, the fans. These are the people you play for. They're a vital part of what drives and motivates you. Focus on those die-hard fans who come to every game rain or shine.

Writing doesn't have to be a solo sport. In fact, if you let them in and make a team effort, you may win more often. It takes all of these to keep you motivated and in the game. When you're feeling low, you seek out your cheerleaders. When you need someone to kick you in the rear, you see the coaches. When you need to talk out a scene or figure out how to word something, you call in another player. And when you need reminding of who's waiting for your story, you just take a look at your fans.

Stay

Focused

AVOID COMMON DISTRACTIONS

Distractions are commonly blamed for causing writer's block. Unless they're inspiring creativity, they need to be eliminated. This is where you have to put on your "I'm the boss around here, guys" hat and live up to your job, Squirrel Herder.

We love them.

Every silly squirrel in the bunch.

But they're all cracked out on caffeine and behaving like a bunch of wasted college kids at a rave. Get ahold of your squirrels! ***Social Media Squirrel*** needs her phone taken away. Instagram, Twitter, Facebook, Snapchat, Tumblr. Enough. I get it. As writers, we need to engage with our readers and keep them interested in our books, but you can't let your online presence take precedence over your book. Focus. Remember your end game here.

Write the book.

"But, K, I can't. Dinner won't make itself. These bills need paying. I need to call Mom."

"K, did you see Chris Pratt's butt on Instagram?"

"Look at that pretty puppy, K."

Are these things that need to be addressed right now, or are they excuses? Are the distractions that are yanking you this way and that necessary at this very moment?

Don't try to write when it's family time or dinner time or bill time or Chris Pratt butt admiring time or puppy petting time. You write during 'writing time', a time that you set aside just for writing. If you aren't putting aside time for this and writing whenever, you are setting yourself up for failure.

Make the time then stick to what you set out to do during said time.

An ongoing joke with my readers and friends is that I "Facebook" when I go to the bathroom. I'll be binge writing all the words, but I have to get up to take breaks. Nature calls. And like any responsible adult of this era, I sit on the commode and scroll through all my social media feeds. Yes, there have been close calls with my phone falling into the toilet. No, I don't forget to wash my hands. Maybe I spend more time on the toilet than is actually necessary. Regardless, I use little breaks of time to pop in and check on my social media so that I'm not using important writing time to scroll aimlessly like some futuristic robotic zombie.

You can do your weird robo-zombie fetish stuff on the toilet.

But the moment that toilet flushes, you're back to work, Squirrel Herder!

Coffee Break—*Identify your most common distractions, and write them down. Are these distractions that can be avoided, or are they ones that are constants like children, pets, or significant others? My most common distractions are Facebook, my daughter, and the doorbell. When it's writing time, I try to ignore my phone no matter how many times it buzzes (because I can totally check on things when all these coffee breaks catch up to me). With my daughter, it's a little more difficult. She has feelings and needs attention—all those things human beings require to be happy...sheesh. I purposefully make sure my writing times are when she's sleeping, playing with her cousins, or at school. Finally, the doorbell. There's nothing worse than being all cozied up—thanks Grammy Loves You Squirrel—writing an intense scene and then DING-DONG! I combat this by hollering for someone else to answer the door or using my new handy dandy door cam. If it's a pesky neighbor, I don't answer the door. If it's UPS, I make a mad dash to the door, collect my*

package of books (because it's always books), then hurry back as quickly as possible, so I don't lose my mojo. Write down your main distractions and when they tend to be the biggest offender. Examine your list to see how these distractions can be best avoided so you can stay in the zone.

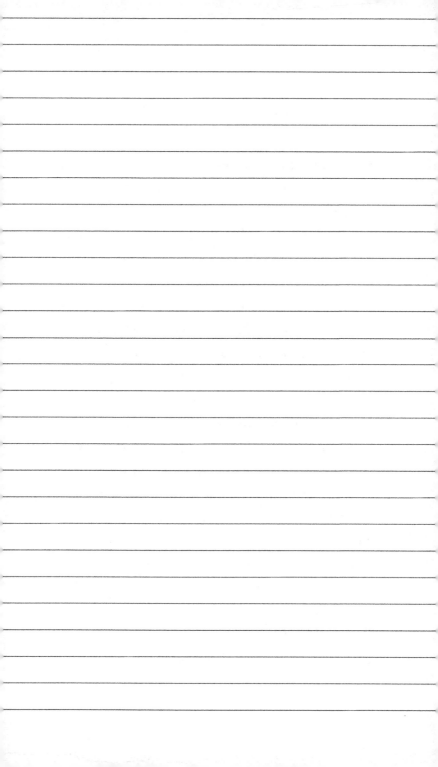

Post or Write?

So, it's toilet Facebook time. You're now allowed to get sucked into all the drama of social media. Right?

Wrong.

This leads to bad habits. Habits that lead you to getting involved in things that continue on past toilet time. Do you really need to get into a twenty comment debate over which is better: ebooks or paperbacks? Spoiler alert, they're both books which means they're both amazing. Whew. Look, I just saved you forty minutes of your life. Here's the thing, social media is addictive. It feeds on our desire to know everything about everyone. Our need to put in our two cents. The never-ending quest to be liked or loved or praised via comments and private messages. You can't let it control you, especially if you're struggling with writer's block. It's easy to get swept up in something you can heatedly type about—something you may feel passionate about. At the end of the day, you sure told them about how nothing compares to the scent of real pages on a paperback, but what do you have to show for that hour? Maybe you didn't engage, but watched the debate unfold.

Are your legs numb yet?

Yeah, I'm talking to you, Squirrel Herder.

Get off the toilet because it's time for real talk.

In an hour, you could have easily written a thousand words. Within a month, using one hour a day that you'd normally be debating something essentially unimportant in the grand scheme of things, you could have 30k words. That's a novella, Squirrel Herder. Imagine if you applied even more time to writing…maybe doubling that time to two hours a day. Oh boy, now you have yourself a novel!

Put down the phone.

People often ask me how I'm able to write so much, and it's because I avoid engaging in social media situations that will distract me. It's easy to get wrapped up in the latest drama or argument, even if it's just watching it all unfold and not commenting at all. You have to learn to turn it off. To not care. It doesn't impact you or your story, so get out of someone else's life and jump back into your own.

Unplug. Back away. Focus.

Think about it as a forced mini vacation. You're not punishing yourself, you're setting yourself free. Rather than being chained to something that continually forces you to compare yourself with others, engage in battles that you wouldn't normally fight in, and seek out highs from virtual strangers, you can unplug and produce.

Post or write?

Don't post. Write. Simple as that.

Go write.

Give yourself that hour or two to focus on your writing, and only compare yourself to the person you were the day before. The dumb viral videos and sassy updates from your friends will be there during toilet time.

You owe it to yourself to take a break.

Trust me when I say you'll learn to crave these breaks. These breaks are peaceful and quiet and aren't threaded with anxiety. You're retraining your brain to look forward to these forced moments away to write. Soon, you'll start demanding more of these breaks for yourself. Pulling away from your phone is not a bad thing.

Your writing is something that makes you happy, and for many of us, provides us with income. Social media can be a curse, stealing time, energy, and potential future money because it's keeping you from doing what you set out to do: write.

Coffee Break—*Put a five-minute timer on your phone. Practice what it feels like to scroll and check on things but not comment, post, or engage. When the timer dings, close the social media app you're in and put your phone in your pocket. Make a cup of coffee, check the mail, or fold some laundry…okay, so that last one is a bit crazy. Just make it your goal to set limits and controls for yourself. You're retraining your brain and making new habits one five-minute bathroom break at a time.*

DON'T ALERT THE PRESS!

After many bouts of trial and error, I realized that pressure is a huge personal block for me when it comes to writing. I get it, it's exciting to tell everyone all about the book you're working on. Sharing quirky scenes and teasers about the characters. While I'm all for that if the book is already written, I would advise against it if you're still writing the story.

"But, K, my readers love teasers. They need to know what I'm working on next."

Yes, Squirrel Herder, I see your point. However, you don't have to use fresh-off-the-press material. Post a snippet of an old book you wrote or recommend a book you're reading and loving.

You must stop telling everyone your move before you make it. That makes you predictable, and with predictability comes demands. Worst of all, it lays a ton of pressure on you. *You promised you were almost done. You promised you loved this book. You promised it would release on my birthday.*

So, where's the book?

That's right, you've pressured yourself into a corner. Your motivation to write is dead. The constant demands have slaughtered your will to finish. Spoiler alert: there is no book.

You've already promised the world your book on a silver platter. It's disappointing and upsetting to both you and your readers if you can't finish the story like you wanted.

Now what?

This habit needs to be broken. You're killing your love of writing, and you're creating an environment of negativity. Why are you so mean to yourself, Squirrel Herder?

Time to rethink your methods. To retrain the brain. Zip those lips.

Meet ***Secret Squirrel***.

Every time you open your mouth, she's there to shove an acorn in it. She reminds you day in and day out of all those times when you teased at a story or started a story only to never finish said story. This sassy squirrel tells you to hush your mouth and get back in the writing cave. Your stories, and especially your plan of action, should remain in a vault until you type "The End."

"Oh no, K. That's not going to work for me. I'm not like you. I love teasing my readers about my stories. We

savvy writers call this 'marketing.' We create buzz before the book comes out. Gah, get a clue."

Hold on. I can't see you. My eyes are still rolling in my head.

Okay, there. I'm now focused on you and the giant ball of pressure you've created all by yourself. Spoiler alert: it's going to flatten you.

Listen, and listen well.

Write the book first.

Just write it.

When it's done, you can holler from the rooftops because you'll be proud. I'll be proud of you too. But no one can be proud of an unfinished story that we've teased our readers about only to realize the characters no longer love us, nor will they ever. You're setting yourself up for disappointment. It may not happen this time or the next time, but eventually it will happen. It happened to me a lot in the beginning of my writing career before I learned that I had to make changes. It was embarrassing and frustrating.

Now, when I don't finish a story, no one knows of my failure.

Or, I admit to my failures in a way that still entertains my readers. Once, I collected all the unfinished stories I'll never complete, slapped them into one manuscript, and gave my readers a published book on Amazon called ***B-Sides and Rarities: A Collection of Unfinished Madness***.

These days, I'm better about protecting my creativity. I'm instantly stifled the moment I put a date on my work. It's one of my own personal writer's block creators. Rather than letting it win, I've learned how to manage and control it by writing my story first, before talking about it.

Simple. As. That.

"But, K, the craze these days is XYZ. My book I'm writing has XYZ in it. I want the readers to see it's coming, so they can be excited."

It's like getting everyone excited that pizza is coming but never getting around to ordering the pizza. We're hungry and angry! We're hangry! Don't tease unless you can 100% deliver the gooey, delicious goods.

Rather than teasing us about what's coming, no matter how confident you are you'll finish, give us a snack of something you've already done. Do any of your other books have any XYZ elements? Could you provide your readers with a delicious snippet of an older book that showcases that exact element everyone is thirsting for at the moment?

Not only will this keep you from threatening

your creativity, it'll reach some new eyes and give some love to an old title. You're still doing your marketing, Squirrel Herder, you're just doing it for a different book.

Keep your unfinished story a secret.

Just do it once and see how it goes.

There's nothing a reader loves more to hear than, "I wrote this book, and I cannot wait for you all to read it." You've got to admit this has a better ring to it than, "I'm writing this book," or, "I'm going to write this book."

Try to think of your book as the spoiler. Don't ruin the experience for your audience by telling them the ending. Let them find that out themselves. When it's done.

I can't stress this enough.

Coffee Break—*Find a key element in your work in progress that you can also find in an older book. Is Hero Harry an arrogant fella like the first hero you created in a book nobody ever reads anymore? Scroll through First Hero's book and find a really juicy scene. Give your readers a little taste in your group. Let them know you're writing something that'll make First Hero seem like a sweetheart. You're giving them a vague tease, letting them know that you're working on something without telling them specifics, while also driving them to that wonderful book that hasn't been getting enough attention. Still trying to write your first book? No problem. Post fun stuff on your writing process, but keep the specifics out of the equation. Example post: "My characters are on fire today, especially my arrogant hero. (Insert vague quote or line). You're in for a real treat with this guy. Details coming soon!"*

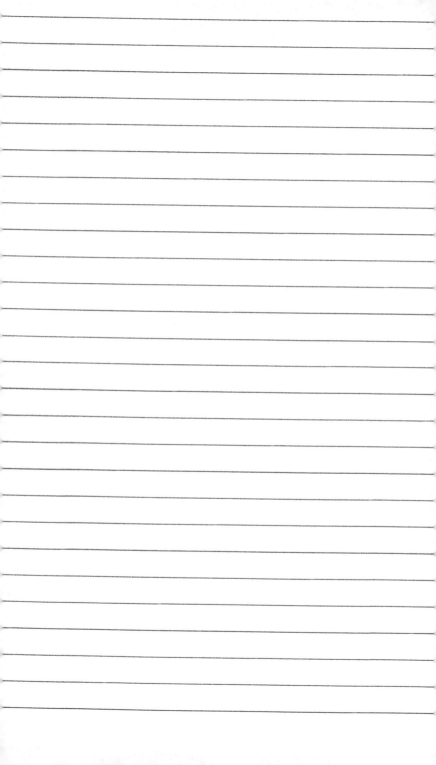

Stick to a Schedule

SCHEDULE

Scheduling is key to being prolific and positively the most important element to take away from this book. You absolutely must carve out consistent times to write during the week and stick to those times. These time slots need to be strictly for writing. As I said before, no lunch dates, paying bills, cleaning the house, or working on marketing. Your scheduled writing time must be only for writing.

"Oh, K, that's wishful thinking. I can only write when I find free time. My life is very busy."

Hear this: Your writing is an integral part of you, and you deserve this time. Pull out your calendar, realistically find times that you can write, and you set those in stone. No penciling times in. Stone. Make this schedule a part of your job, and view it as important as actually going to your real job or picking your kids up from school. It needs to start to become a routine for you.

When I started scheduling my writing, I produced more yet also spent more time with my family.

"Impossible, K!"

Listen, Squirrel Herder, I know what I'm talking about. My kids, during the regular school year, are in school a good chunk of the week. I've set aside Mondays and Fridays to take care of bookkeeping, housekeeping, online book orders, marketing, etc. The weekend is mine to do whatever I want. But Tuesday through Thursday? Those are my scheduled writing days. By the time I get home from dropping off my kids, set my scene, and sit down to write it's around ten. The night before, I try to read up on the book I'm going to write to get the juices flowing so that the next day, I can dive straight into writing. I use those hours, until I have to pick up my kids around two, strictly for writing. Sometimes I pause to heat up a Lean Cuisine or eat a bowl of cereal. Sometimes I starve. But I keep my distractions to a minimum and take very few breaks.

Why?

Because that is my writing time.

I only get three days, which doesn't feel like enough. Four hours, three days a week doesn't seem like much, but since it's my dedicated writing time, I try to write between 5-10k words each day. At the very minimum, if I write 15k words a week for those three days, that's 60k in a month. So, at the very minimum, I'm completing one book a month. Often, I write more than that and sneak in extra writing times as rewards. We'll talk about writing rewards in another chapter.

"K, I work a full-time job, am the only one who cooks or cleans at my house, and have friends outside of the virtual world. When I write, I only have one hour of time after everyone goes to bed."

Great. That's awesome. Now you need to carve out those times and assign them a spot on your calendar. Don't make it willy-nilly in your head. Actually write it down in that one hour slot each night. Even if you only write 1k words during that hour, three days a week, that's 12k words in a month. It's going to feel good, consistently getting those words down, and you'll begin to carve out more time for yourself.

This book isn't about making excuses for why you can't write. This book is about learning how other people manage their writing time, and how they achieve consistent word counts so that maybe you can pick up some tips to implement for yourself.

An hour a day is such a small amount of time to dedicate to what you love. People spend countless hours on their hobbies and jobs all the time. You have to start demanding this time for yourself. Develop a routine with your family. Let them know when you're working, and train them to fend for themselves during that time. It may not go according to plan at first, but with time and effort, you'll develop a routine just like anything else in your life.

With any new endeavor, you'll have hiccups along the way. Inevitably, nine emergencies will pop up within your household during your scheduled writing time. However, eventually everyone will get used to this time. If you have children, this might be once they go to bed. Give yourself some flexibility to fine tune those times, but also be firm with those around you who demand your time. People thrive on routine. All that's stopping you is you.

Coffee Break—*Look at your calendar right now, and realistically find slots for your writing. Make it a priority to discuss with your family how you are going to take those times to write and that you'll need to be undisturbed. Once you've carved out your slots, try to think about what you can accomplish during that time, and project what that will look like by the end of the month.*

Make Attainable Goals

Everyone wants to write as many words as they possibly can. We're storytellers, and the time we spend on our manuscripts never feels like enough. However, with a schedule, goals, and a plan, you can achieve what you want rather easily.

Goals can either be motivators or destroyers. I've been that person who made impossible goals for herself only to be disappointed one month in when I realized I'd never meet said goals. It was then I began to change my mindset on goals. With writing, it's no different. Yes, I want to write 100k words each month. Will I? Probably not. Your writing goals need to be flexible and changeable.

"K, you just told me to keep my writing schedule set in stone! Now you're telling me to get my pencil out to try and erase it?"

I'm telling you to keep your schedule written in stone, but keep your goals loose. For instance, I aim for four hours a day, three days a week. Ideally, I can write for twelve hours a week. If I write 1500 words in an hour (give or take, depending on how in the zone I am), that's 18k a week. Then, multiply that by four weeks and I've got 72k words!

Rather than assuming I'll never get interrupted, never have a headache, feel uninspired, or be called away from those set-in-stone times for writing, I plan for half the productivity. I'd rather smash my goal than fall sadly below it. 36k words feels like an easy goal to me, one that I'll blow through without much thought.

Here's the thing about goals.

When we smash one, we get pumped up and eager to smash another.

So, when the middle of the month rolls around and I'm sitting at 36k words completed, I throw myself a party—the squirrels get to have their rave—and then I see if I can hit 40k because that's just 4k more. When I hit 40k, then I aim for 45k. I keep at this until the end of the month. Next thing I know, I've written close to (and sometimes surpass) my original goal of 72k. Now, had I aimed for 72k to begin with, it would have felt too far away. Too intimidating. Too large. And if I didn't make it there and only reached 68k, I'd have felt let down and disappointed in myself, never mind the fact that 68k words in a month is a really good number.

It's about reprogramming your mind. While this tactic makes me a horrible gambler at the casino—*just five more bucks and I'll hit big*—it makes goal smashing easy. If I start hitting 60k words a month consistently, then I might slowly increase my goal to beat the month before. Like I said in the beginning of this book, I'm in a constant competition with myself. I see these numbers day in and day out. Only I can compare who I was yesterday to who I am today.

By following the easy tips in this book, you can truly transform your output. It may start slow, but with time, you can build on what you've learned and practice what works. Your goals are fluid and changeable. As you learn about what works for you, you can modify your goals. Become a little better, quicker, and more focused than the person you were yesterday. Goals and accountability go hand in hand. Tracking your numbers every day and being accountable with what you write each day keeps your goals right in your face, so you don't conveniently forget them.

Coffee Break—*Spend an hour writing (if you didn't already do the coffee break in the Accountability section) to determine an average word count for yourself. Setting aside a time to track and know your ability is important in discovering your average, so don't pass up this exercise. Now, based on your set-in-stone writing times and your average word count, what do you think you could accomplish in that time? Write that figure down. Multiply it out over the month. Next, divide that number in two and make it your monthly goal. If the number overwhelms you, divide it by two again and look at it as a weekly goal. For one week, I want you to work hard on smashing that goal.*

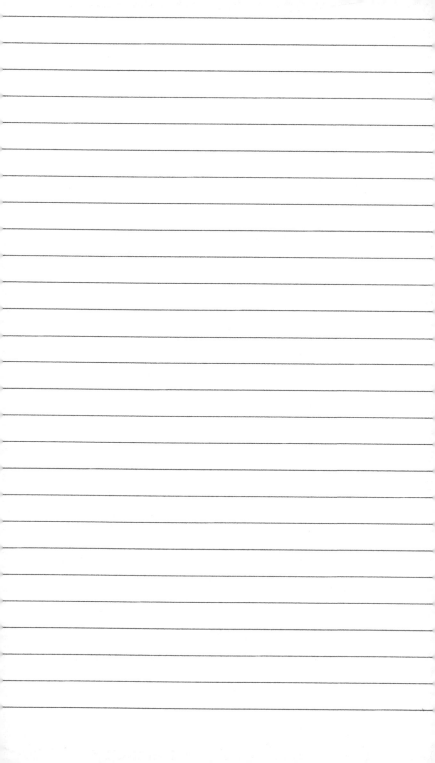

REWARD YOURSELF

With every goal in life, there should be an incentive to achieve more, higher goals. As humans, we thrive on this. It's a great process. But I'm about to rock your world for a minute because I'm about to change your way of thinking…again.

Before you go shopping for that new guitar (if you're my husband), that new pair of shoes (if you're my daughter), or that new video game (if you're my son), stop. Just pull the brakes for one second.

You're not going to reward yourself with things (or brownies in my case).

"K, I wrote 36k words this month! I deserve to reward myself with a manicure, a night binge-watching Game of Thrones *reruns, or a friggin' trip to Sonic for a cherry limeade. Come on! Don't let me down now!"*

Go on. Throw your fit for a minute and when you calm down, let's have real talk.

Better now?

Meet ***Passion Project Squirrel***.

This squirrel is the one who gets shoved aside a

lot. She's quiet and patient, but beautiful and worthy. She sits there while you finish your chores and your obligations. This sweet squirrel listens to all your empty promises about how you'll give her attention one day. When you forget about her, she forgives you anyway. Squirrel Herder, you've let her down. It's time to pull her from the shadows, and let her play a little.

We've all been here. At the point where we've made plans to do all these projects, losing sight of some stuff we really want to do if only we had the time.

Here's where I rock your world.

Passion Project Squirrel is your reward. Not the cold, cherry and lime goodness from Sonic's limeade. Not a friggin' brownie (I'm looking at myself on this one). Not a purchase or a movie night or a walk with the dog.

You have to start rewarding writing with writing.

You've smashed your goal, so that gives you time to "play." When we discuss the **Four Bouncing Balls Method**, I'll get more into your passion project and where this falls. For now, let's talk about your reward.

Everyone has that book that they've always wanted to write. Maybe it's a short story about aliens. It could be a how-to manual, a cookbook, a spicy romance, or a thriller. It could be something that's the complete opposite of what you write now, or it could be a character from one of your other novels you've always felt deserved a story. Whatever it is, that's your reward. If you don't have a passion project, you're going to find one. This needs to be something that is strictly because you *want* to write it, not because it is on the agenda.

Now, each week, when you blow through your goals for your "have-to" projects, you get to use those set-in-stone hours to write your passion project. It's something you can look forward to.

I have implemented this myself and have written many of my passion projects over the years. These books—because they're filled with absolute love and fueled by desire to write them rather than duty—have turned out to be some of my most successful stories. That's the goal here. To avoid writer's block and be more prolific. Being prolific doesn't have to be an obligation. It can be fun too.

I can promise that once you start doing this, writing will become much more exciting. We're tricking the way we think, remember? Right now, you're probably blocked most days because you dread having to work on your obligation. Why?

Often, it's because deep down, you feel guilty for ignoring Passion Project Squirrel. You're torn between doing what needs to be done and what you want to do. Once you start using your passion project as your reward, you can change the whole game. You're rewarding yourself with more writing. Productivity increases right alongside with your happiness. This is something you can easily do, and frankly, it's something you deserve.

Coffee Break—*Identify your passion project. Allow yourself a moment (outside of your set-in-stone writing time) to think about the story and plot. Make a quick outline. Finally, open a Word document and name it. I'll explain what to do with this open document in the next section, but whatever you do, don't close it. For now, I want you to determine this project and set it up. If it's already something you've started, open it. Our rewards should be within reach, and our goals should be attainable. You're almost there.*

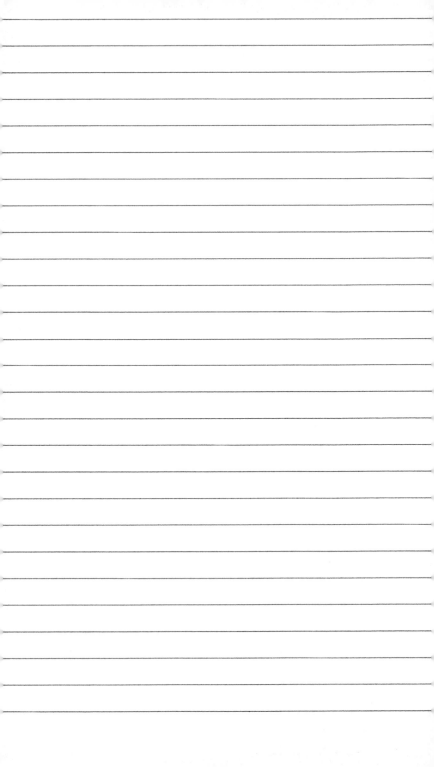

Stay
Productive

FOUR BOUNCING BALLS METHOD

Here's where we get into the nitty gritty on how I personally stay moving continuously. I've published over eighty stories. Everything from novellas to long books to series. I've published aliens and thrillers and historical romances and dark and everything in between. Some months, I published two and three stories. Other months, just one. My personal goal is to continually publish something each month. I've developed a system that works for me. It's called the Four Bouncing Balls Method.

Imagine you're at a restaurant and you see one of those quarter machines. Inside are all these pretty bouncing balls. You have four quarters, so you purchase four balls—each distinct and unique from the others. Now, unless you can juggle like Harry Styles—*don't ask questions about my boy band obsession, just go with it*—it'll be difficult to play with all four balls at once. The moment you try, they all go bouncing everywhere. One gets lost, you have to chase down the others. It's exhausting, and not much fun.

But guess what? There's a way to play with them all, essentially, all at once. It takes practice and a little coordination, but soon you'll be skilled at this.

Drop the first ball. Take a step, drop the next ball. Another step, another drop. And finally, step aside, and drop the last ball. Watch them all bouncing in unison beside each other. Pretty and fascinating, I agree.

Now think of these balls as your manuscripts.

"K! Four manuscripts open at once? Absolutely not! That's chaos!"

Remember, Squirrel Herder, you're not playing with all four at once. You're bouncing them individually, letting them bounce side by side, admiring all of them. You can pull one from the line at any given moment to play with it while the other three continue to bounce.

Focus and listen.

You can do this. You have your obligation book, maybe you have two or three works in progress. That's great. We want them all open and ready. And that final glittery ball? That's your passion project. Feels nice to see it rather than think it, huh?

For me, I always, ***always*** have multiple documents open at once. I've co-written with multiple authors, and that's what birthed this process in the first place. I hated sitting idly while I waited for my co-writer to finish their part of the project. Additionally, whenever I'd get writer's block, I loathed sitting still, doing nothing. Thus, the Four Bouncing Balls Method was born.

What happens when you've unsuccessfully tried to decompress, remove distractions, or inspire yourself on Pinterest? What happens when you schedule, plan, and make goals but the words for your extremely necessary work in progress simply won't come to you?

Usually, that's when you go on Facebook, go online shopping, or wonder about the inner workings of the space time continuum. Not anymore. It's time to retrain your brain. You're going to find projects to keep open, so that you can always, ***always*** be writing during your set-in-stone times.

And here's where we bounce.

You're stuck on a scene, you've tried everything, and it still won't budge. Easy. Toggle and open the next document, preferably one that's been calling to you. Get cracking! The point of this method isn't to confuse the ever-loving stew out of you, it's to keep the proverbial ball rolling—or bouncing in our case. Every stalled minute on your current WIP should be another minute of progress on a different project.

Out of four choices, your brain will select the one it prefers. And rather than fighting what it wants, give in. It's win-win. You're happy, and you're slamming down words rather than twiddling your thumbs.

I get it. It's confusing at first. You're going to have to organize your thoughts and learn to compartmentalize. I know it can be done because I do it every day and have been for years. I write all over the map in different genres.

Coffee Break—*Write down your four projects. Your WIP, your passion project, and two more. Maybe two are old books that you started yet stopped for various reasons. Maybe they're two more passion projects, or maybe they're books that are next up in line after your WIP. Whatever they are, I want you to list them out. Seeing them helps you visualize and form a plan. You need to read over your notes to familiarize yourself with each story and open documents so they're ready. If the story is old or you've forgotten it, in a not set-in-stone writing time, read through these books to get the vibe thrumming through you again. Keep them saved and open at all times. Next time you stall on your WIP, I want you to dabble in one of them, and see if you can continue writing. This is an exercise that will take practice. It'll be clunky and awkward to begin with, but soon, you'll learn to use it as a crutch when you're feeling blocked. A crutch that has purpose and maintains your productivity.*

In a Nutshell...

HERE'S A QUICK RECAP TO HELP YOU REMEMBER!

Identifying Your Problem

Identify why you're stuck. Distract. Decompress.
Squirrel Herder.
Ooh, That's Pretty! Squirrel.

Making a Plan

Brainstorm. Break it down. Organize. Set the Scene.
Brainstorming Betsy Squirrel.
Bang-Bang Squirrel.
Grammy Loves You Squirrel.

Being Accountable

Track your words. Find accountability partners.
All-Star Squirrel. (And don't forget his cheerleaders, coaches, teammates, and fans!)

Staying Focused

Avoid common distractions like social media. Don't alert the press.
Social Media Squirrel. Secret Squirrel.

Sticking to a Schedule

Schedule Writing Time. Make attainable goals. Reward yourself with writing.
Passion Project Squirrel.

Staying Productive

Four Bouncing Balls Method.

OUTRO

Being an author can be hard work. Publishing, marketing, graphics, social media, newsletters. We tend to drown in the author part and lose focus of the writing part. Writing is the most important part, though. You can't sell good books unless you write them first. I hope you'll take what you learned from this book and use it to help you stay focused and on track. Remember, Squirrel Herder, you're in charge. It's time to show those wild squirrels who's boss and make them work for you!

Now that you've taken a short pause to analyze your writing habits and work on ways to improve them, it's time to hit the play button and get back to work! Good luck, and thank you for reading! If you found this book helpful, please leave a review!

Have a question for Squirrel Queen, K Webster? You can email here or visit her Facebook page to shoot a message there.

Looking for the book K mentioned about the compilation of unfinished works called *B-Sides and Rarities: A Collection of Unfinished Madness*? You can find it on Amazon.

Don't forget to download the K Webster's *Paused to Prolific* Word Count Tracker for free!

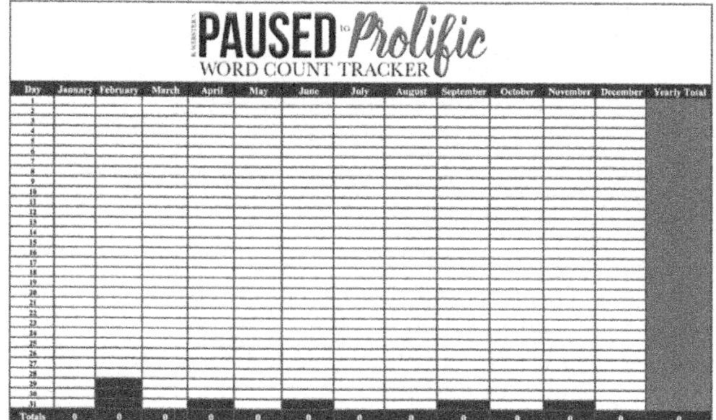

K WEBSTER'S PAUSED to Prolific
WORD COUNT TRACKER

Day	January	February	March	April	May	June	July	August	September	October	November	December	Yearly Total
1													
2													
3													
4													
5													
6													
7													
8													
9													
10													
11													
12													
13													
14													
15													
16													
17													
18													
19													
20													
21													
22													
23													
24													
25													
26													
27													
28													
29													
30													
31													
Totals	0	0	0	0	0	0	0	0	0	0	0	0	0

BOOKS BY K WEBSTER

Psychological Romance Standalones:

My Torin

Whispers and the Roars

Cold Cole Heart

Blue Hill Blood

Wicked Lies Boys Tell

Romantic Suspense Standalones:

Dirty Ugly Toy

El Malo

Notice

Sweet Jayne

The Road Back to Us

Surviving Harley

Love and Law

Moth to a Flame

Erased

Extremely Forbidden Romance Standalones:

The Wild

Hale

Like Dragonflies

Taboo Treats:

Bad Bad Bad

Coach Long

Ex-Rated Attraction

Mr. Blakely

Easton

Crybaby

Lawn Boys

Malfeasance

Renner's Rules

The Glue

Dane

Enzo

Red Hot Winter

Dr. Dan

KKinky Reads Collection:

Share Me

Choke Me

Daddy Me

Watch Me

Hurt Me

Play Me

Contemporary Romance Standalones:

Wicked Lies Boys Tell

The Day She Cried

Untimely You

Heath

Sundays are for Hangovers

A Merry Christmas with Judy

Zeke's Eden

Schooled by a Senior

Give Me Yesterday

Sunshine and the Stalker

Bidding for Keeps

B-Sides and Rarities

Conheartists

Paranormal Romance Standalones:

Apartment 2B

Running Free

Mad Sea

Cold Queen

War & Peace Series:

This is War, Baby (Book 1)

This is Love, Baby (Book 2)

This Isn't Over, Baby (Book 3)

This Isn't You, Baby (Book 4)

This is Me, Baby (Book 5)

This Isn't Fair, Baby (Book 6)

This is the End, Baby (Book 7 – a novella)

LOST PLANET SERIES:

The Forgotten Commander (Book 1)

The Vanished Specialist (Book 2)

The Mad Lieutenant (Book 3)

The Uncertain Scientist (Book 4)

The Lonely Orphan (Book 5)

The Rogue Captain (Book 6)

2 LOVERS SERIES:

Text 2 Lovers (Book 1)

Hate 2 Lovers (Book 2)

Thieves 2 Lovers (Book 3)

PRETTY LITTLE DOLLS SERIES:

Pretty Stolen Dolls (Book 1)

Pretty Lost Dolls (Book 2)

Pretty New Doll (Book 3)

Pretty Broken Dolls (Book 4)

THE V GAMES SERIES:

Vlad (Book 1)

Ven (Book 2)

Vas (Book 3)

FOUR FATHERS BOOKS:

Pearson

FOUR SONS BOOKS:

Camden

Elite Seven Books:

Gluttony

Greed

Royal Bastards MC:

Koyn

Truths and Lies Duet:

Hidden Truths

Stolen Lies

Books Only Sold on K's Website and Eden Books:

The Wild

The Free

Hale

Bad Bad Bad

This is War, Baby

Like Dragonflies

The Breaking the Rules Series:

Broken (Book 1)

Wrong (Book 2)

Scarred (Book 3)

Mistake (Book 4)

Crushed (Book 5 – a novella)

The Vegas Aces Series:

Rock Country (Book 1)

Rock Heart (Book 2)

Rock Bottom (Book 3)

The Becoming Her Series:

Becoming Lady Thomas (Book 1)

Becoming Countess Dumont (Book 2)

Becoming Mrs. Benedict (Book 3)

Alpha & Omega Duet:

Alpha & Omega (Book 1)

Omega & Love (Book 2)

ABOUT AUTHOR K WEBSTER

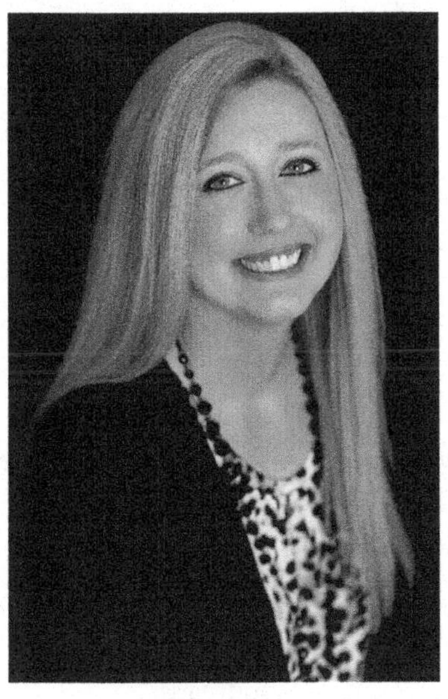

K Webster is a *USA Today* Bestselling author. Her titles have claimed many bestseller tags in numerous categories, are translated in multiple languages, and have been adapted into audiobooks. She lives in "Tornado Alley" with her husband, two children, and her baby dog named Blue. When she's not writing, she's reading, drinking copious amounts of coffee, and researching aliens.

Keep up with K Webster

Website:
www.authorkwebster.com

Email:
kristi@authorkwebster.com

Facebook:
www.facebook.com/authorkwebster

Twitter:
twitter.com/KristiWebster

Goodreads:
www.goodreads.com/user/show/10439773-k-webster

Instagram:
www.instagram.com/authorkwebster

BookBub:
www.bookbub.com/authors/k-webster

ACKNOWLEDGEMENTS

For the sake of not making the acknowledgements longer than the book, I'd like to quickly thank those who are always in my circle. Matt Webster, Nicole Blanchard, Stacey Blake, Kim BookJunkie, Elizabeth Clinton, Ella Stewart, Misty Walker, Holly Sparks, Jillian Ruize, Gina Behrends, Wendy Rinebold, J.D. Hollyfield, Ker Dukey, and Nikki Ash—you all are amazing!

And a huge thank you to all of the wonderful readers out there! I can't thank you enough for your ongoing support and enthusiastic readership!

Made in the USA
Monee, IL
30 May 2020

32224519R00079